dump & bake
Cakes

Guide to Cake Mixes

✧ 1 *(9 x 13")* or 2-layer size cake mix: 15.25 to 18.25 oz. pkg. *(3⅓ to 4 cups dry cake mix)*

✧ 1 *(8" or 9")* size cake mix: 9 oz. pkg. or half a *(9 x 13")* pkg. *(scant 2 cups dry cake mix)*

✧ Homemade cake mix *(recipes on pages 62-63)*: Use 3⅓ to 4 cups mix to replace 1 *(9 x 13")* size package or scant 2 cups mix to replace 1 *(8" or 9")* size package.

✧ Angel food: 16 oz.

Printed in the United States of America
by G&R Publishing Co.

Distributed By:

Products

507 Industrial Street
Waverly, IA 50677

ISBN-13: 978-1-56383-433-2
ISBN-10: 1-56383-433-2
Item #7078

The beauty of dump cakes is their simple, no-fuss, no-muss preparation. A dry cake mix and a few simple ingredients are layered in a baking dish and popped into the oven. Butter or other liquids on top combine with fruit juices from the bottom to moisten the cake mix like magic.

Helpful Hints

✧ Break up any lumps in the dry cake mix.

✧ Spread layers evenly for uniform baking.

✧ Pour liquid ingredients slowly and evenly over the cake mix to avoid dry spots. Mix lightly, if desired.

✧ Butter may be added in three different ways: sliced, grated or melted. Choose the method you like best, but be sure butter is well chilled if slicing or grating.

✧ Use purchased cake mixes or prepare homemade ones (recipes on pages 62-63).

✧ Drizzle additional melted butter or other liquid over any dry areas during baking, or spritz with butter spray during the last 15 minutes of baking time.

✧ To reduce calories, replace some of the butter with juice, water or diet soda, or use fresh fruit instead of pie filling. (Note: Angel food cakes work best with regular soda.)

✧ Let cakes cool at least 30 minutes before serving. Most can be successfully refrigerated overnight.

Serve dump cakes warm or cold, with or without add-ons like ice cream, whipped cream, powdered sugar or frosting. Experiment with different fruits to find your favorite combinations. Whether scooped or cut, dump cakes make a sweet and easy dessert every time!

Orange Dreamsicle

1 (18.25 oz.) pkg. orange cake mix

1 (3.4 oz.) pkg. French vanilla instant pudding mix

2 (11 oz.) cans mandarin oranges, juice reserved

Orange juice

3 eggs

½ C. cold butter, thinly sliced

½ C. butter cookie crumbs, optional

Preheat oven to 325°.
Lightly grease a 9 x 13" baking dish.

Layers

✧ Dump dry cake mix and pudding mix in a mound in prepared baking dish. Make a well in the center of dry ingredients.

✧ Combine reserved juice from mandarin oranges with enough orange juice to measure 1½ cups liquid. Add eggs and juice mixture to well and whisk together until well-blended, scraping down sides.

✧ Stir in mandarin oranges and spread batter evenly in dish.

✧ Arrange butter slices over the top. Sprinkle with cookie crumbs, if desired.

Bake

about 45 minutes or until cake tests done with a toothpick. Cool completely.

Try

spreading whipped topping over the cake. Chill before slicing.

Pineapple-Cherry

1 (20 oz.) can crushed pineapple, drained
1 (21 oz.) can cherry pie filling
1 (9 oz.) pkg. yellow cake mix
½ C. chopped pecans
5 T. butter, melted

Preheat oven to 350°.
 Lightly grease an 8 x 8˝ baking dish.

ℒayers

✦ Spread pineapple in prepared
   baking dish.

✦ Cover pineapple with cherry
   pie filling.

✦ Sprinkle dry cake mix evenly
   over fruit.

✦ Scatter pecans over the top.

✦ Drizzle melted butter over all.

Bake

40 to 45 minutes or until
   golden brown.

Serves
15

Black Cherry Rhubarb

4 C. chopped fresh rhubarb

½ C. sugar

1 (3 oz.) pkg. black cherry gelatin

1 (18.25 oz.) pkg. white or yellow cake mix

⅓ C. butter, melted

1 C. water

Preheat oven to 350°.
*** Lightly grease a 9 x 13″ baking dish.***

Layers

✧ Arrange rhubarb in prepared
   baking dish.

✧ Sprinkle sugar and dry gelatin
   over rhubarb.

✧ Dump dry cake mix in a mound on
   rhubarb mixture. Make a well in
   the center of cake mix. Slowly pour
   melted butter and water into well.

✧ Without disturbing rhubarb, stir
   gently until mostly blended.

Bake

about 45 minutes or until
   golden brown and bubbly.

German Chocolate

1 (18.25 oz.) pkg. German chocolate cake mix

3 eggs

1 C. water

1 C. sweetened flaked coconut

¾ C. chopped pecans

¾ C. sweetened condensed milk

Preheat oven to 300°.
Lightly grease a 9 x 13" baking dish.

Layers

✧ Dump dry cake mix in a mound in prepared baking dish. Make a well in the center of cake mix and add eggs and water. Whisk ingredients together until well blended; scrape down sides and spread evenly.

✧ Sprinkle coconut over cake batter.

✧ Scatter pecans over the top.

✧ Drizzle sweetened condensed milk evenly over all.

Bake

40 to 50 minutes or until cake tests done with a toothpick.

Peach Cobbler

1 (16 oz.) pkg. frozen sliced peaches
1 T. cornstarch
1 tsp. vanilla extract
¼ C. brown sugar
½ tsp. ground cinnamon
1 (9 oz.) pkg. white or yellow cake mix
½ C. honey and oats granola
¼ C. butter, melted

Lightly grease a
  2½- to 3-quart slow cooker.

Layers

✧ Place peaches in prepared slow
  cooker. Sprinkle with cornstarch
  and toss lightly.

✧ Drizzle with vanilla.

✧ Sprinkle with brown sugar
  and cinnamon.

✧ Sprinkle dry cake mix and
  granola evenly over the top.

✧ Drizzle with melted butter.

Cook

  covered 3 to 3½ hours on high setting.

 **Try**

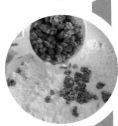

*frozen boysenberries in place of
peaches or 2 cups homemade spice
cake in place of white or yellow cake.*

*Use a slow cooker for other recipes in this book
by following basic directions given here.*

Pineapple-Mango Angel

2 C. chopped fresh mango (about 2 mangoes)*
1 (20 oz.) can crushed pineapple, undrained
1 (16 oz.) pkg. angel food cake mix
2 (6 oz.) cans pineapple juice (1½ C.)
Butter spray

* You may also use chopped frozen mango, thawed.

Preheat oven to 350˚.
  Lightly grease a deep 9 x 9˝ baking dish.

Layers

✦ Arrange mango in prepared
   baking dish.

✦ Spread pineapple over mango.

✦ Sprinkle dry cake mix evenly
   over fruit.

✦ Drizzle juice over the top.

Bake

55 to 60 minutes, spritzing
   dry areas with butter spray
   and covering lightly with foil
   after 40 minutes to prevent
   overbrowning. Cool completely
   before serving.

Serves
15-20

Lemon Pineapple

1 (21 oz.) can lemon pie filling
1 (20 oz.) can crushed pineapple, undrained
Zest from 1 lemon
1 (18.25 oz.) pkg. lemon cake mix
1 C. butter, melted
1 C. sweetened flaked coconut
¾ to 1 C. chopped macadamia nuts

Preheat oven to 350°.
Lightly grease a 9 x 13" baking dish.

Layers

✧ Spread lemon pie filling in prepared baking dish.

✧ Spread pineapple over pie filling. Sprinkle with lemon zest.

✧ Sprinkle dry cake mix evenly over fruit.

✧ Drizzle melted butter over the top.

✧ Sprinkle coconut and macadamia nuts evenly over all.

Bake

50 to 55 minutes. Cover with foil the last 15 minutes to prevent overbrowning.

Cherry Cheesecake

1 (21 oz.) can cherry pie filling

1 (12 oz.) pkg. frozen sweet cherries

6 oz. Neufchâtel-style cream cheese

1 (18.25 oz.) golden vanilla cake mix

½ C. lemon-lime soda

½ C. cold butter, thinly sliced

1 C. graham cracker crumbs

Preheat oven to 350°.
  Lightly grease a 9 x 13˝ baking dish.

Layers

- ✦ Spread cherry pie filling and frozen cherries in prepared baking dish.
- ✦ Drop teaspoonful-size pieces of cream cheese over cherries.
- ✦ Sprinkle dry cake mix evenly over cream cheese layer.
- ✦ Drizzle lemon-lime soda over all.
- ✦ Top with butter slices.
- ✦ Sprinkle with graham cracker crumbs.

Bake

30 to 40 minutes or until golden brown and bubbly around edges.

Caramel Apple

1 (21 oz.) can apple pie filling

1 (9 oz.) pkg. yellow cake mix

2 T. brown sugar

½ C. apple juice

½ C. chopped honey-roasted
   peanuts or cashews

¼ C. butter, melted

Preheat oven to 350°.
Lightly grease a 9 x 9˝ baking dish.

Layers

✧ Spread apple pie filling in prepared baking dish.

✧ Sprinkle dry cake mix and brown sugar evenly over pie filling.

✧ Drizzle apple juice over dry ingredients.

✧ Sprinkle with peanuts.

✧ Drizzle melted butter over all.

Bake

40 to 45 minutes. Cool completely before serving.

topping with whipped cream and drizzling with caramel sauce.

All-American

1 (21 oz.) can red raspberry, strawberry
  or cherry pie filling

1 C. fresh or frozen blueberries, thawed

1 (9 oz.) pkg. white cake mix

½ C. finely chopped pecans

½ C. butter, melted

Preheat oven to 325 °.
  Lightly grease an 8 x 8˝ baking dish.

Layers

- ❖ Spread raspberry pie filling in prepared baking dish.
- ❖ Arrange blueberries over pie filling.
- ❖ Sprinkle dry cake mix evenly over fruit.
- ❖ Sprinkle with pecans.
- ❖ Drizzle melted butter over all.

Bake

45 to 50 minutes or until golden brown and bubbly.

Pumpkin Pie Crunch

1 (29 oz.) can pumpkin puree

3 eggs, lightly beaten

1 (12 oz.) can evaporated milk

1¼ C. sugar

2 to 3 tsp. ground pumpkin pie spice

1 (18.25 oz.) pkg. yellow cake mix

1 C. graham cracker crumbs

½ C. toffee bits

1 C. butter, melted

Preheat oven to 350°.
Lightly grease a 9 x 13˝ baking dish.

Layers

✧ Dump pumpkin puree, eggs, evaporated milk, sugar and pumpkin pie spice into prepared baking dish. Stir ingredients together until well blended; scrape down sides and spread evenly.

✧ Sprinkle dry cake mix evenly over pumpkin mixture.

✧ Sprinkle with graham cracker crumbs. Scatter toffee bits over the top.

✧ Drizzle melted butter over all.

Bake

50 to 55 minutes or until cake is lightly browned and tests done with a toothpick. Cool before serving. Refrigerate overnight, if desired.

Key Lime

3 eggs

⅓ C. water

1 (19.35 oz.) pkg. Krusteaz Key Lime
   Bars mix, divided

1 (9 oz.) pkg. yellow cake mix

½ C. sweetened condensed milk

¼ C. butter, melted

¼ C. sliced almonds, optional

Preheat oven to 350°.
  Lightly grease an 8 x 8˝ baking dish.

Layers

✧ Dump eggs, water and key lime filling
   from Krusteaz mix into prepared dish.
   Whisk together until blended; let rest
   10 minutes to thicken.

✧ Stir thickened lime mixture in dish
   and scrape down sides. Sprinkle
   dry cake mix evenly over the top.

✧ Drizzle with sweetened condensed milk.

✧ Sprinkle at least half of crumb
   topping from Krusteaz mix over
   the top.

✧ Drizzle melted butter over all.
   Sprinkle with almonds, if desired.

Bake

40 to 50 minutes or until lightly
   browned. Cool completely; chill at
   least 2 hours. Let stand at room
   temperature 30 minutes before slicing.

*drizzling with a key lime juice
and powdered sugar glaze.*

27

Apple-Pear-Carrot

1 (15.25 oz.) can diced pears, undrained
1 (21 oz.) can apple pie filling
½ C. raisins, optional
1 (15.25 oz.) pkg. carrot cake mix
½ C. sweetened flaked coconut
½ C. chopped walnuts or pecans
½ C. butter, melted

Preheat oven to 350°.
   Lightly grease a 9 x 13″ baking dish.

Layers

✧ Reserve 2 to 3 tablespoons pear
   juice. Dump pears and remaining
   juice into prepared baking dish.
   Spread apple pie filling over pears,
   mixing lightly. Sprinkle with raisins,
   if desired.

✧ Sprinkle dry cake mix evenly over fruit.

✧ Scatter coconut over the top.

✧ Sprinkle with walnuts.

✧ Drizzle melted butter and reserved
   pear juice over all.

Bake

about 45 minutes, reducing
   oven temperature to 325°
   after 10 minutes.

drizzling thinned cream cheese
frosting over cool cake before serving.

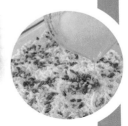

29

Rhubarb Lite

1 (15.25 oz.) pkg. vanilla cake mix
1 (12 oz.) can diet lemon-lime soda (1½ C.)
4 C. chopped fresh rhubarb
1 C. granulated Splenda sweetener (or sugar)
2 tsp. ground cinnamon
½ C. fat-free half & half
Butter spray, optional

Preheat oven to 350°.
Lightly grease a 9 x 13″ baking dish.

Layers

- ✧ Dump dry cake mix and lemon-lime soda into prepared baking dish; stir until well combined. Scrape down sides and spread evenly.
- ✧ Arrange rhubarb over cake batter.
- ✧ Sprinkle with Splenda and cinnamon.
- ✧ Drizzle half & half over all.

Bake

40 to 45 minutes or until cake tests done with a toothpick. To enhance browning, spray cake with butter spray partway through baking time, if desired.

Fresh Blackberry

4 C. fresh blackberries*

⅓ C. sugar

1 (3 oz.) pkg. blackberry or raspberry gelatin

1 (18.2 oz.) pkg. golden butter cake mix

½ C. quick-cooking rolled oats

½ C. chopped pecans

½ C. butter, melted

1½ C. water

Preheat oven to 350°.
  Lightly grease a 9 x 13˝ baking dish.

ℒayers

- ✧ Arrange blackberries in prepared baking dish.

- ✧ Sprinkle sugar and dry gelatin over berries.

- ✧ Sprinkle dry cake mix evenly over berry mixture.

- ✧ Scatter oats and pecans over the top.

- ✧ Drizzle with melted butter. Then slowly pour water over all.

Bake

40 to 45 minutes or until lightly browned and cake tests done with a toothpick.

* You may also use frozen blackberries, thawed and well-drained.

Fresh Nutty Apple

5 C. peeled, thinly sliced apples

1 T. lemon juice

1 (15.25 oz.) pkg. French vanilla cake mix

½ C. sugar

2½ tsp. ground cinnamon, divided

¼ tsp. ground nutmeg

½ C. apple juice or cider

½ C. cold butter

½ C. chopped pecans

Preheat oven to 350°.
  Lightly grease a 9 x 13˝ baking dish.

Layers

✧ Place apples in prepared baking
   dish. Sprinkle with lemon juice
   and toss lightly; spread evenly.

✧ Spread dry cake mix evenly
   over apples. Sprinkle sugar,
   2 teaspoons cinnamon and
   nutmeg over cake mix. Drag
   a fork through dry ingredients
   to mix lightly.

✧ Drizzle with apple juice.

✧ Grate butter evenly over the top.

✧ Sprinkle pecans and remaining
   ½ teaspoon cinnamon over all.

Bake

40 to 50 minutes or until apples are
   tender and top is golden brown.

Banana Split

1 (20 oz.) can crushed pineapple, undrained

2 bananas, diced

1 (18.25 oz.) pkg. white cake mix

1 (21 oz.) can strawberry pie filling

1 C. diet lemon-lime soda

Preheat oven to 325°.
Lightly grease a 9 x 13″ baking dish.

Layers

✧ Dump pineapple and bananas into prepared baking dish. Toss together and spread evenly.

✧ Spread half the dry cake mix evenly over fruit (about 2 cups).

✧ Drop spoonfuls of strawberry pie filling evenly over cake mix.

✧ Sprinkle remaining dry cake mix over pie filling.

✧ Drizzle lemon-lime soda over the top, and without disturbing fruit, stir gently until mostly blended.

Bake

55 to 60 minutes or until cake tests done with a toothpick. To enhance browning, increase oven temperature to 350° for last 10 minutes of baking.

Try

topping with whipped cream, chocolate sauce and/or a maraschino cherry.

Lemon Blueberry

1 (18.25 oz.) pkg. lemon supreme cake mix

1 (3.4 oz.) pkg. vanilla instant pudding mix

3 eggs

1 (12 oz.) can Mountain Dew or lemon-lime
soda (1½ C.)

1¾ C. fresh or frozen blueberries, thawed

8 lemon sandwich cookies, crushed
(about 1 C. crumbs)

Preheat oven to 325°.
Lightly grease a 9 x 13″ baking dish.

Layers

- ✧ Dump dry cake mix and pudding mix into prepared baking dish.
- ✧ Make a well in the center of dry ingredients; add eggs and Mountain Dew. Whisk together until well blended, scraping down sides.
- ✧ Stir in blueberries and spread batter evenly.
- ✧ Sprinkle cookie crumbs over the top.

Bake

45 to 50 minutes or until cake tests done with a toothpick.

drizzling with white icing.

Black Forest

2 (21 oz.) cans cherry pie filling, divided

1 C. crushed chocolate wafer crumbs
(about 15 wafers)

1 (16.5 oz.) pkg. devil's food cake mix

½ C. cold butter, thinly sliced

½ C. chopped maraschino cherries, optional

½ C. maraschino cherry juice, optional

Preheat oven to 350°.
Lightly grease a 9 x 13˝ baking dish.

Layers

✧ Spread one can cherry pie filling in prepared baking dish.

✧ Sprinkle wafer crumbs over pie filling. Spread remaining can pie filling over crumb layer.

✧ Sprinkle dry cake mix evenly over pie filling.

✧ Arrange butter slices over all. (For brownie-like texture, scatter maraschino cherries over the top and drizzle with cherry juice.)

Bake

55 to 60 minutes.

Try

stirring chopped, drained maraschino cherries into whipped topping. Place a dollop on each serving and sprinkle with shaved chocolate.

Cranberry Lemon

5 to 6 C. fresh or frozen cranberries, thawed

1 C. sugar

2 C. boiling water

1 (15.25 oz.) pkg. lemon supreme cake mix

1 C. chopped walnuts, pecans or granola

½ C. butter, melted

Preheat oven to 350°.
Lightly grease a 9 x 13˝ baking dish.

Layers

◇ Spread cranberries in prepared
   baking dish. Sprinkle with sugar.

◇ Pour boiling water over cranberries
   and let stand 5 to 10 minutes.

◇ Spread dry cake mix evenly over
   cranberry mixture.

◇ Sprinkle with walnuts.

◇ Drizzle melted butter over all.

Bake

45 to 50 minutes or until golden
brown and bubbly around edges.

Peachy Butter Pecan

1 (29 oz.) can sliced peaches, undrained

1 (15.25 oz.) pkg. butter pecan cake mix

1 C. chopped pecans

1 C. sweetened flaked coconut

½ C. butter, melted

½ C. toffee bits, optional

Preheat oven to 325°.
  Lightly grease a 9 x 13″ baking dish.

Layers

✧ Dump peaches into prepared
  baking dish.

✧ Spread dry cake mix evenly
  over peaches.

✧ Sprinkle with pecans and coconut.

✧ Drizzle melted butter over all.

✧ Scatter toffee bits over the top,
  if desired.

Bake

about 50 minutes or until golden
  brown and bubbly around edges.

S'mores

1 (15.25 oz.) pkg. milk chocolate cake mix

3 eggs

1 C. water

2¼ C. mini marshmallows, divided

½ C. graham cracker crumbs

⅔ C. mini milk chocolate chips

Preheat oven to 325°.
Lightly grease a 9 x 13″ baking dish.

Layers

- ✧ Dump dry cake mix, eggs and water into prepared baking dish. Whisk together until well blended, scraping down sides.

- ✧ Stir in 1 cup marshmallows; spread evenly.

Bake

until almost done, about 20 minutes. Sprinkle graham cracker crumbs, chocolate chips and remaining 1¼ cups marshmallows over top of cake and bake 10 minutes more or until cake tests done with a toothpick. Place under broiler for 1 to 2 minutes, just long enough to toast marshmallows.

Serves
9

Strawberry-Apple Angel

1 (21 oz.) can strawberry pie filling

2 C. peeled, grated apples

1 T. lemon juice, optional

1 (16 oz.) pkg. angel food cake mix

1¼ C. apple juice

Butter spray, optional

Preheat oven to 350°.
  Lightly grease a 9 x 9˝ baking dish.

Layers

✧ Spread strawberry pie filling in
   prepared baking dish.

✧ Arrange grated apples over
   pie filling; sprinkle with lemon
   juice, and without disturbing pie
   filling, toss lightly.

✧ Sprinkle dry cake mix evenly over fruit.

✧ Drizzle apple juice over all.

Bake

about 60 minutes, spritzing dry
  areas with butter spray halfway
  through baking time, if desired.
  To prevent overbrowning, cover
  lightly with foil after 30 minutes.

Apricot Spice

1 (15.25 oz.) pkg. spice cake mix

3 eggs

1 (21 oz.) can apricot pie filling

1 (16 oz.) container cream cheese frosting*

Preheat oven to 350°.
Lightly grease a 9 x 13˝ baking dish.

Layers

- ✧ Dump dry cake mix in a mound in prepared baking dish and make a well in the center.
- ✧ Add eggs and apricot pie filling; stir until well blended, scraping down sides.
- ✧ Spread batter evenly.

Bake

25 to 30 minutes or until cake springs back when lightly touched. Cool completely. Spread cream cheese frosting over the top.

* Or prepare homemade cream cheese frosting by beating together 3 ounces softened cream cheese and 6 tablespoons softened butter. Beat in 1 teaspoon milk, 2 teaspoons vanilla and 1¾ cups powdered sugar until smooth and creamy.

Peach-Mandarin Orange

1 (29 oz.) can sliced peaches, drained

1 (11 oz.) can mandarin oranges, drained

1 (15.25 oz.) can sliced pears, drained

½ to 1 tsp. ground cinnamon

⅓ C. brown sugar

1 (18.25 oz.) pkg. yellow cake mix

1 (12 oz.) can orange soda (1½ C.)

3 T. cold butter, sliced

Preheat oven to 350°.
Lightly grease a 10˝ Dutch oven.

Layers

✧ Arrange peaches, mandarin oranges and pears evenly in prepared Dutch oven. Sprinkle with cinnamon and stir gently to mix.

✧ Sprinkle brown sugar over fruit.

✧ Dump dry cake mix in a mound on fruit and make a well in the center.

✧ Pour orange soda into well, and without disturbing fruit, stir gently to blend. Spread batter evenly.

✧ Arrange butter slices over the top. Leave Dutch oven uncovered for oven baking.

Bake

about 1 hour in the oven or until cake tests done with a toothpick. If cooking outdoors, cover Dutch oven and set on a ring of 9 or 10 hot coals; place remaining hot coals on lid. Cook for 45 to 60 minutes, rotating pot and lid several times during cooking.

Use a Dutch oven for other recipes in this book by following basic directions given here.

Tropical Fruit

2 (15 oz.) cans tropical fruit, undrained

1 (11 oz.) can mandarin oranges, juice reserved

½ C. chopped maraschino cherries, drained

3 T. brown sugar

1 (18.25 oz.) pkg. pineapple cake mix

1 C. honey and oats granola

½ C. slivered almonds

¼ C. sweetened flaked coconut, optional

½ C. butter, melted

Preheat oven to 350°.
Lightly grease a 9 x 13″ baking dish.

Layers

✧ Spread tropical fruit, mandarin oranges and cherries evenly in prepared baking dish. Sprinkle with brown sugar.

✧ Spread dry cake mix evenly over fruit.

✧ Scatter granola and almonds over the top.

✧ Sprinkle with coconut, if desired.

✧ Drizzle with reserved mandarin orange juice and melted butter.

Bake

about 50 minutes or until golden brown and bubbly.

Try

substituting two cans fruit cocktail for the tropical fruit.

Orange Chocolate Truffle

1 (15 oz.) can mandarin oranges, drained

2 T. juice and zest from 1 orange

2¾ C. dry chocolate cake mix*

¼ C. fat-free half & half

¼ C. orange soda

½ C. semi-sweet chocolate chips

5 T. melted butter

* Use part of a standard cake mix, reserving
extra for another use.

Preheat oven to 350°.
  Lightly grease an 8 x 8˝ baking dish.

Layers

❖ Spread mandarin oranges in prepared
    baking dish; add orange juice and
    sprinkle with orange zest.

❖ Sprinkle dry cake mix evenly
    over fruit.

❖ Drizzle half & half and orange
    soda over cake mix, and without
    disturbing oranges, mix lightly
    until partially blended.

❖ Sprinkle chocolate chips over the top.

❖ Drizzle with melted butter.

Bake

30 to 35 minutes or until set.

Try

sprinkling cooled cake with
powdered sugar and additional
orange zest, or mix a little dry
orange gelatin into whipped topping
and let stand 30 minutes before
spooning onto servings.

Strawberry Pretzel

1 (8 oz.) tub whipped cream cheese

2 T. sugar

1 (21 oz.) can strawberry pie filling

1 (9 oz.) pkg. white cake mix

2 T. dry strawberry gelatin

½ C. kiwi-strawberry juice

¼ C. cold butter

½ C. crushed pretzels

Preheat oven to 325°.
Use an ungreased 8 x 8˝ baking dish.

Layers

✧ Spread cream cheese over bottom of baking dish. Sprinkle with sugar.

✧ Cover evenly with strawberry pie filling.

✧ Spread dry cake mix evenly over pie filling. Sprinkle with dry gelatin and drag a fork through dry ingredients to mix lightly.

✧ Drizzle with kiwi-strawberry juice, and without disturbing pie filling, stir gently until partially blended.

✧ Grate butter evenly over the top.

Bake

50 to 60 minutes or until lightly browned. Scatter pretzels over cake halfway through baking time.

Try

topping with whipped cream, additional crumbled pretzels and/or a sliced strawberry.

Chocolate Fudge-Raspberry

2 (21 oz.) cans red raspberry pie filling

Zest from 1 lemon, optional

1 (16.5 oz.) pkg. dark chocolate cake mix

1 C. baking chips (semi-sweet and/or white
   chocolate chips)

¾ C. butter, melted

Preheat oven to 350°.
Lightly grease a 9 x 13" baking dish.

Layers

- ✧ Spread raspberry pie filling in prepared baking dish. Lightly sprinkle with lemon zest, if desired.
- ✧ Sprinkle dry cake mix evenly over pie filling.
- ✧ Scatter baking chips over cake mix.
- ✧ Drizzle melted butter over all.

Bake

40 to 50 minutes. Cover lightly with foil toward end of baking time to prevent overbrowning.

serving warm over ice cream.

Homemade Cake Mixes

Prepare homemade cake mixes to use in place of packaged cake mixes listed in recipes, if desired. For convenience, make a large batch ahead of time and store in airtight container(s) until needed.

Big Batch Homemade White Cake Mix

Makes enough for 3 (9 x 13") or 6 (8" or 9") cakes

7½ C. sifted flour

4½ C. sugar

1 T. salt

2 T. baking powder

¾ C. cold butter, cut into small pieces

In a very large bowl, whisk together flour, sugar, salt and baking powder until well blended. Place butter in a food processor container and add 2 cups flour mixture. Cover and process until mixture is very fine and butter is evenly distributed. Return to bowl and whisk together with remaining flour mixture.

Divide cake mix into three equal portions (about 4 cups each) by lightly scooping mixture into 1-quart jars or zippered plastic bags. Refrigerate for up to one month or freeze for up to 3 months. Use one portion in place of 1 (9 x 13") packaged white or yellow cake mix or use 2 cups dry mix in place of 1 (8" or 9") packaged cake mix as directed in recipes.

To make a single batch, use 2½ cups sifted flour, 1½ cups sugar, 1 teaspoon salt, 2 teaspoons baking powder and ¼ cup butter. Follow directions above, using just 1 cup flour with butter in food processor. Use in place of 1 (9 x 13") packaged white or yellow cake mix as directed in recipes.

Quick Homemade Chocolate Cake Mix

1 (4-cup) portion dry
   homemade white cake mix
   (recipe page 62)

3 to 4 T. unsweetened
   cocoa powder

In a large bowl, whisk together dry white cake mix and cocoa powder until blended. Use in place of 1 (9 x 13") packaged chocolate cake mix as directed in recipes.

Quick Homemade Spice Cake Mix

1 (4-cup) portion dry
   homemade white cake mix
   (recipe page 62)

1 tsp. ground cinnamon

½ tsp. ground nutmeg

⅛ tsp. ground cloves

⅛ tsp. ground allspice

In a large bowl, whisk together dry white cake mix, cinnamon, nutmeg, cloves and allspice until blended. Use in place of 1 (9 x 13") packaged spice cake mix as directed in recipes.

Single Batch Homemade Yellow Cake Mix

Makes enough for 1 (9 x 13") or 2 (8" or 9") cakes

2 C. flour

1½ C. sugar

1 T. baking powder

½ C. nonfat dry milk powder

2 tsp. vanilla extract

In a large bowl, whisk together flour, sugar, baking powder and milk powder until blended. Store in an airtight container at room temperature. Use in place of 1 (9 x 13") packaged yellow cake mix as directed in recipes, adding vanilla with the liquid ingredients.

Index